# Buzzing b Words

bird    bell    ball    baby    book    boy

Read the clues to finish the puzzle.

## Across

1. The ___ flew away.
2. What time does the class ___ ring?
3. We have a new ___ in our class.

## Down

1. Let's play ___ after school.
2. Give the ___ her toy.
3. The ___ is about animals.

# Rhyming With c Words

| car | coat | cake | corn | cook | candy |

Read the clues to finish the puzzle.

## Across

1. I rhyme with boat.
2. I rhyme with horn.
3. I rhyme with make.

## Down

1. I rhyme with sandy.
2. I rhyme with look.
3. I rhyme with far.

# Rhyming With d Words

duck    down    draw    doll    dish    dark

Read the clues to finish the puzzle.

## Across

1. I rhyme with wish.
2. I rhyme with town.
3. I rhyme with park.

## Down

1. I rhyme with saw.
2. I rhyme with luck.
3. I rhyme with fall.

**down**

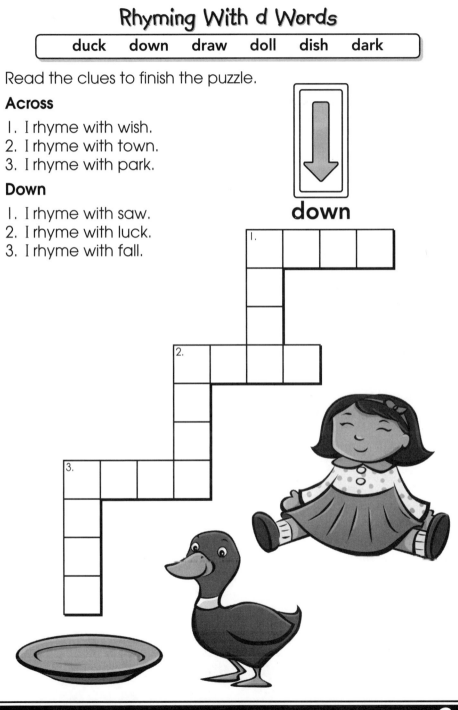

# Fabulous f Words

| flower | fire | five | fox | frog | fish |

Read the clues to finish the puzzle.

## Across

1. The dog looks like a ___.
2. Billy is ___ years old today.
3. A ___ has long back legs.

## Down

1. The firemen put out the ___.
2. A rose is a pretty ___.
3. ___ live in water.

# Great g Words

| green | gift | grapes | girl | goat | gum |
|-------|------|--------|------|------|-----|

Read the clues to finish the puzzle.

## Across

1. What is the name of the new ___ at school?
2. Jason wore a ___ t-shirt.
3. The ___ was for my birthday.

## Down

1. ___ are my favorite fruit.
2. A ___ is a farm animal.
3. Do not chew ___ in school.

# Happy h Words

| hat | house | happy | hook | hen | heart |

Read the clues to finish the puzzle.

## Across

1. Hang your coat on the ___.
2. Amy drew a ___ shape on the paper.
3. Our ___ lays eggs.

## Down

1. Wear a ___ when it is cold outside.
2. We moved to a new ___.
3. Grandmother is ___ to see us.

# Rhyming with j Words

| jam | jump | jeep | jeans | jog | jacks |

Read the clues to finish the puzzle.

## Across

1. I rhyme with ham.
2. I rhyme with beans.
3. I rhyme with bump.

## Down

1. I rhyme with sacks.
2. I rhyme with deep.
3. I rhyme with dog.

# Rhyming with K Words

| kite | kitten | keep | kind | kiss | kick |

Read the clues to finish the puzzle.

## Across

1. I rhyme with sick.
3. I rhyme with find.
4. I rhyme with deep.

## Down

1. I rhyme with mitten.
2. I rhyme with miss.
3. I rhyme with bite.

# Lively l Words

Read the clues to finish the puzzle.

## Across

1. What tree has this kind of ___?
2. A ___ is a small reptile.
3. The ___ looks like a big cat.

## Down

1. A ___ is needed to reach up high.
2. A ___ is a yellow fruit.
3. Turn on the ___.

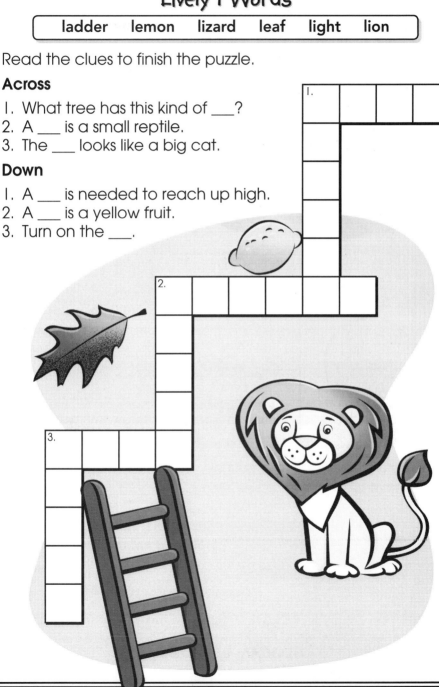

# Merry m Words

mittens    monkey    mouse    money    moon    map

Read the clues to finish the puzzle.

## Across

1. The ___ ran under the bed.
2. I keep my ___ in the bank.
3. I can see the ___ at night.

## Down

1. The ___ ate the banana.
2. ___ keep my hands warm.
3. A ___ shows where we live.

# Nifty n Words

| number | nest | nickel | nurse | nine | nuts |

Read the clues to finish the puzzle.

## Across

1. There are five pennies in a ___.
2. The ___ worked with the doctor.
3. Squirrels eat ___.

## Down

1. A ___ tells how many.
2. Birds lay eggs in a ___.
3. I saw ___ ducks swimming.

# Perfect p Words

pink    pretty    puppy    play    penny    pick

Read the clues to finish the puzzle.

## Across

2. Who did you ___ for the team?
3. A ___ is a baby dog.

## Down

1. ___ is a color.
2. A ___ is 1¢.
3. Let's ___ ball!
4. Flowers are very ___.

Please don't pick the daisies.

# Quaint q Words

| question | quilt | quail | quarter | queen | quiz |

Read the clues to finish the puzzle.

**Across**

1. A ___ is a quick test.
2. Mom put a pretty ___ on my bed.
3. I could not answer the ___.

**Down**

1. A ___ is a kind of small bird.
2. There are five nickels in a ___.
3. A ___ rules her country.

# Restful r Words

| rain | read | road | ring | rope | robot |

Read the clues to finish the puzzle.

## Across

1. We used a ___ to pull the sled.
2. The ___ made us wet and cold.
3. I like to ___ books about animals.

## Down

1. Did you hear the bells ___?
2. Take this ___ to our house.
3. A ___ can do work for us.

# Super s Words

| stars | seven | stop | soap | socks | sing |

Read the clues to finish the puzzle.

## Across

1. ___ are very bright at night.
3. Wash your hands with ___.
4. Mom likes to ___ while working.

## Down

1. Can you make the dog ___ barking?
2. Beth will be ___ years old tomorrow.
3. Did your shoes and ___ get wet?

# Tasteful t Words

| talk | take | today | toys | tall | tell |
|------|------|-------|------|------|------|

Read the clues to finish the puzzle.

**Across**

2. The baby is beginning to ___.
3. Dolls and balls are kinds of ___.
4. Can you ___ me a story?

**Down**

1. How long did the test___?
2. ___ is my birthday.
3. Hank is ___ for his age.

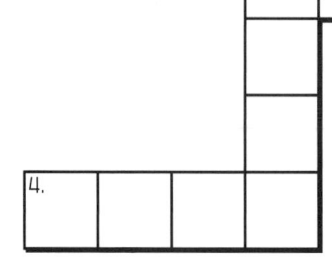

# Valuable v Words

| valentine | van | vest | vase | vine | violin |

Read the clues to finish the puzzle.

## Across

2. Amy is taking ___ lessons.
3. The ___ is growing over the fence.
4. I wore a ___ to keep me warm.
5. Put the flowers in the ___.

## Down

1. A ___ is somewhat like a truck.
2. I sent a ___ to my best friend.

# Wise w Words

| wolf | water | wheel | wagon | worm | watch |

Read the clues to finish the puzzle.

## Across

2. I gave my puppy a ride in my ___.
3. The ___ of my bike needs to be oiled.
4. A ___ crawled onto the sidewalk.

## Down

1. A ___ is a wild animal.
2. My ___ is ten minutes slow.
3. All living things need ___ to live.

# Fantastic x, y, and z Words

| x-ray | yellow | yard | zero | zipper | zebra |
|-------|--------|------|------|--------|-------|

Read the clues to finish the puzzle.

## Across

2. We planted flowers in our front ___.
3. The score was four to ___.
4. A ___ has black and white stripes.

## Down

1. An ___ is a picture of what's inside of something.
2. My favorite color is ___.
3. The ___ on my coat is silver.

# Short a Words

| rabbit | map | ant | mask | apple | rat |

Read the clues to finish the puzzle.

## Across

1. A ___ looks like a large mouse.
2. An ___ is an insect.
3. A ___ helps us find roads.

## Down

1. A ___ can be a good pet.
2. I like ___ pie.
3. We all wore a ___ at the Halloween party.

# Short e Words

| dress | sled | cent | nest | seven | tent |
|-------|------|------|------|-------|------|

Read the clues to finish the puzzle.

## Across

2. I wore my new ___ today.
4. A robin built a ___ in our tree.
6. A penny is one ___.

## Down

1. We rode our ___ down the snowy hill.
3. ___ is my lucky number.
5. We slept in our ___ last night.

# Short i Words

| dish | kick | kiss | chick | pig | ship |

Read the clues to finish the puzzle.

## Across

2. The ___ fell and broke.
3. He gave the ball a hard ___.
4. A ___ is a very large boat.

## Down

1. A ___ is a young chicken.
3. I gave Mother a ___ goodbye.
5. A young hog is called a ___.

# Short o Words

| clock | sock | lock | spot | hot | block |

Read the clues to finish the puzzle.

## Across

2. The pen made an ink ___ on her dress.
4. The ___ is five minutes fast.
5. Make sure you ___ the door.

## Down

1. The soup is too ___ to eat.
2. I have a hole in my ___.
3. My friend lives a ___ away from me.

# Short u Words

| truck | jump | drum | puppy | duck | funny |

Read the clues to finish the puzzle.

## Across

2. We saw a ___ swimming in the pond.
3. I had to ___ over the puddle.
5. Harry tells ___ jokes.

## Down

1. A ___ can carry things too big for a car.
2. I play a ___ in the band.
4. A ___ is a young dog.

# Short Vowel Review

sun    egg    pig    sock    ten    hat

Read the clues to finish the puzzle.

## Across

2. Which word has the same vowel sound as dock?
3. Which word has the same vowel sound as men?
5. Which word has the same vowel sound as dig?

## Down

1. Which word has the same vowel sound as sat?
2. Which word has the same vowel sound as fun?
4. Which word has the same vowel sound as leg?

# Long a Words

| train | plane | whale | rain | play | hay |

Read the clues to finish the puzzle.

## Across

3. We left the picnic when it began to ___.
4. Another word for airplane is ___.
5. ___ is food for animals.

## Down

1. A ___ moves on tracks.
2. A ___ is not a fish.
4. Our school is putting on a ___.

# Long e Words

| clean | leave | money | meat | tree | seed |

Read the clues to finish the puzzle.

## Across

2. We had to ___ the party early.
3. I did not have enough ___ to buy it.
5. The ___ is losing its leaves.

## Down

1. ___ is the opposite of dirty.
3. ___ is a kind of food that comes from animals.
4. A ___ has a tiny plant inside it.

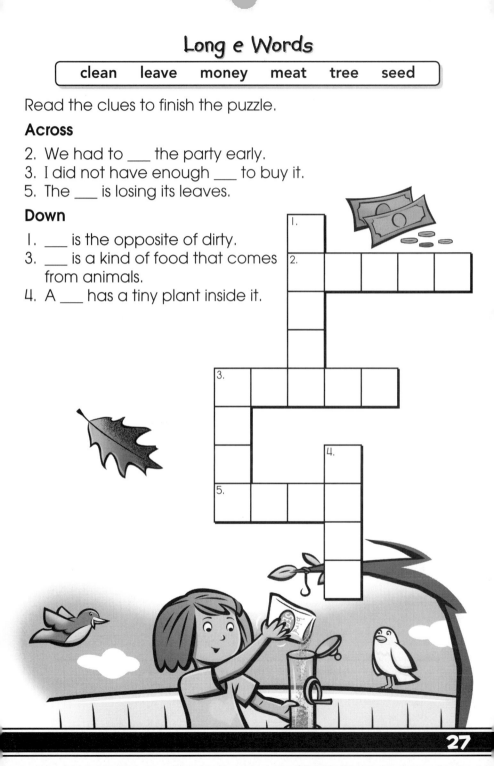

# Long i Words

| nine | kite | hive | white | night | bike |

Read the clues to finish the puzzle.

## Across

2. A color opposite of black is ___.
4. One more than eight is ___.
5. I can fly my ___ on a windy day.

## Down

1. My ___ has a flat tire.
3. Bees live in a ___.
4. The opposite of day is ___.

# Long o Words

| toad | snow | road | crow | toast | ghost |

Read the clues to finish the puzzle.

## Across

2. I like to have ___ when I eat eggs.
4. We drove home on a bumpy ___.
5. White flakes of ___ fell all day.

## Down

1. A ___ is a scary shape in stories.
2. A ___ looks something like a frog.
3. A ___ is a big, black bird.

# Long u Words

| mule | fruit | blue | ruler | glue | tube |

Read the clues to finish the puzzle.

## Across

2. A ___ belongs in the horse family.
3. Apples and oranges are ___.
5. My favorite color is ___.

## Down

1. A ___ helps me measure length.
4. Most toothpaste comes in a ___.
6. Hold the pages together with ___.

# Long Vowel Review

| kite | tube | bee | bone | slide | rake |

Read the clues to finish the puzzle.

## Across

1. This word has the long a sound.
4. This word has the long u sound.
6. This word has the long i sound.

## Down

2. This word has the long i sound.
3. This word has the long e sound.
5. This word has the long o sound.

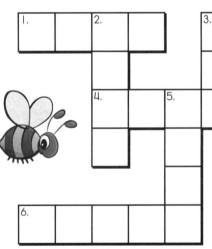

# Synonyms

| small | leave | glad | same | like | end |
|-------|-------|------|------|------|-----|

Read the clues to finish the puzzle.

## Across

1. I mean the same as little.
3. I mean the same as go.
5. I mean the same as happy.

## Down

1. I mean the same as alike.
2. I mean the same as enjoy.
4. I mean the same as stop.

# Nouns

| rabbit | penny | moon | town | mother | pear |

Read the clues to finish the puzzle.

## Across

1. A coin worth one cent is a ___.
2. A ___ is sometimes called a bunny.
4. We can see the ___ in the sky at night.

## Down

1. A ___ is a fruit.
3. A ___ is smaller than a city.
4. A woman who has a child is a ___.

# Rhyming Words

| mouse | bake | block | sack | spin | nest |

Read the clues to finish the puzzle.

## Across

2. It rhymes with lake.
3. It rhymes with back.
4. It rhymes with best.

## Down

1. It rhymes with house.
2. It rhymes with clock.
3. It rhymes with twin.

# Homophones

| sail | sale | write | right | there | their |

Read the clues to finish the puzzle.

## Across

2. Is your answer ___?
4. Put the book over ___.
5. The store is having a ___ on shoes.

## Down

1. Can you ___ your name?
3. They like ___ new home.
5. Where did you ___ your new boat?

# Opposites

old    short    down    night    slow    near

Read the clues to finish the puzzle.

## Across

1. The opposite of new is ___.
3. The opposite of fast is ___.
4. The opposite of day is ___.

## Down

2. The opposite of up is ___.
3. The opposite of long is ___.
4. The opposite of far is ___.

# Verbs

| jump | play | hurry | help | paint | talk | kick |

Read the clues to finish the puzzle.

## Across

1. How high can you ___?
3. I was late and had to ___.
4. What color should we ___ the house?
6. How far did he ___ the ball?

## Down

2. Let's ___ ball!
3. Will you ___ me fix dinner?
5. He gave a short ___ about pets.

# Reptiles

| alligator | gecko | lizard | snake | turtle |

Read the clues to finish the puzzle.

## Across

1. A ___ does not have legs.
4. A ___ looks somewhat like a snake.
5. A ___ is a lizard that can walk upside down.

## Down

2. An ___ has very powerful jaws.
3. A ___ is a reptile that has a shell.

# Weather

| sunny | rainy | foggy | cloudy | snowy | windy |

Read the clues to finish the puzzle.

## Across

2. It is a ___ day, so I am going to the beach.
4. A cloud near the ground makes it ___.
5. I use an umbrella when it is ___.

## Down

1. Things blow away when it is ___.
2. I wear a hat and mittens when it is ___.
3. You can't see the sun when it is ___.

# Transportation

| plane | bus | train | truck | ship | car |

Read the clues to finish the puzzle.

## Across

2. I rhyme with slip.
4. I rhyme with rain.
5. I rhyme with star.

## Down

1. I rhyme with us.
3. I rhyme with drain.
4. I rhyme with duck.

# Birthday Party

cake     games     gifts     candles     balloons     invitation

Read the clues to finish the puzzle.

## Across

2. An ___ invites us to a party.
3. There will be ___ to play.
4. ___ will be blown out.

## Down

1. ___ float above.
3. We give nicely wrapped ___.
4. Then we eat ___!

# Birds

| robin | owl | duck | ostrich | bluebird | hawk |

Read the clues to finish the puzzle.

## Across

1. This bird can be someone's name.
3. This bird can be found near water.
4. We can see this bird at the zoo.

## Down

2. This bird has a color word in its name.
4. You can hear this bird asking, "Who?"
5. This is a bird of prey.

# Toys

| blocks | kite | boat | ball | doll | drum |

Read the clues to finish the puzzle.

## Across

1. The stack of ___ fell down.
3. I lost the sail to my new___.
4. Keisha likes to dress her ___ in jeans.

## Down

2. The ___ flew into a tree.
3. The ___ rolled under the chair.
4. A ___ makes a booming sound.

# Pets

| fish | hamster | bird | dog | cat | turtle |

Read the clues to finish the puzzle.

**Across**

3. I look like a mouse.
5. I am "man's best friend."
6. I run after mice.

**Down**

1. I like to swim.
2. I have feathers.
4. I have a hard shell.

# Farm Animals

| horse | pig | sheep | goose | goat | cat |
|-------|-----|-------|-------|------|-----|

Read the clues to finish the puzzle.

## Across

2. Which animal gives us wool?
5. Which animal has feathers?
6. Which animal likes to chase mice?

## Down

1. Which animal do we ride?
3. Which animal likes to roll in mud?
4. Which animal has horns?

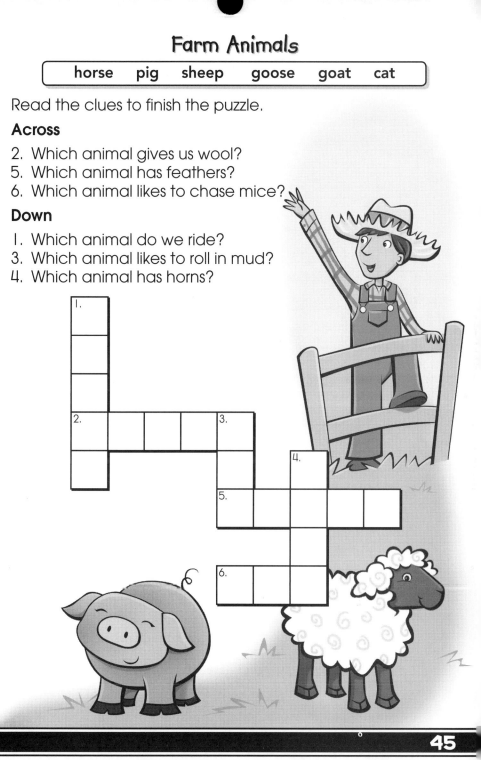

# Colors

| blue | orange | green | yellow | brown | red |

Read the clues to finish the puzzle.

## Across

1. What color rhymes with "true"?
3. What color is made with yellow and red?
4. What color rhymes with "seen"?

## Down

1. What color rhymes with "clown"?
2. What color rhymes with "Jell-o"?
5. What color rhymes with "bed"?

# Fruits

| orange | grapes | pear | lemon | banana | apple |

Read the clues to finish the puzzle.

**Across**

1. I am also the name of a color.
3. I am long and yellow.
5. I rhyme with "bear."
6. I am used to make a tart drink.

**Down**

2. I grow in bunches.
4. Would you like a slice of ___ pie?

# Positional Words

| down | under | between | bottom | middle | over |
|------|-------|---------|--------|--------|------|

Read the clues to finish the puzzle.

## Across

2. The number five is ___ four and six.
4. Do you have a ___ name?
5. A jet flew ___ my house.

## Down

1. Jack and Jill fell ___ the hill.
2. The soap sank to the ___ of the tub.
3. The mouse ran ___ the bed.

up